The Top Mistakes You Make In Your Finances

By

Benny Ferguson Jr.

The Top Mistakes You Make In Your Finances
By Benny Ferguson © 2014

ISBN:
978-1-7354117-6-7

Published by:
The Ferguson Company

Editor & cover design:
http://roxanec.wix.com/time-to-read.com

Welcome

The idea of money is a realm that few ever surmount. They fail to realize that it is not the money that should be the focus. It is the mechanism that draws the money to you that should be the focus. Then there is the issue of self-worth, the ultimate money deterrent. Where do you fall in the area of money? Are you clear on the damaging ideas you carry and their effects on your life? The equation for money is not money for money, it is value for value.

Being Emotionally Attached To Money – Unit Of Exchange

"Your money," is the mistake. It is not yours. Money is merely a mechanism of exchange between two people or entities for services rendered. The more important your service appears to be in the mind of another, the more money they will give you in exchange for it. There is no emotion involved. There is no attachment. There is no love, hate, happy or sad. There is no anxiety, guilt, shame, or need for forgiveness. It is a means of exchange, nothing more. Thank you!

The problem with money in your life is not the money. It is the level of service you have chosen to provide and the worth that you bring to bear with that service. If you provide a service in which you may easily be replaced then you do not command a large unit of exchange for your service. However, if you provided a service in which you couldn't be replaced at all, then you would receive large sums for it.

So how do you position yourself to be a recipient of large sums of money if that is your goal? First is to find what you are excited and passionate about, and allow the service you provide to personify and display the emotion and passion you feel for the service you're about to deliver. The energy you exude from this position propels your attractive forces outward and guarantees your success. It is systematic. It is routine. It has always occurred this way, and will occur for you.

Emotion toward money has never been a determining factor. Emotion toward the service you provide has always been a factor.

Key:

Remove all emotion swirling around and toward money. The flow, the possession of, and or a lack of money have nothing to do with money itself, and everything to do with you the being who is human for a brief moment. Negative emotion shuts off the flow. Fear and anxiety strangles the flow, even if you are in line with your soul's service. Become the provider of a unique service, a service that only you can provide the way that you provide it. Market it to those that want it and provide excellent customer service. This is your path to wealth.

Direct Reflection Of Your Self-Worth, Possibility

The reflective nature of life takes no back seat when it comes to your finances. Any true deliverer of massive service and value knows that you must first believe in yourself. There is no escape from the trap of unworthiness, until you realize that you exist from the Source of all things. With your very existence being a firm case for the delivery of all that you desire, whatever you undertake has success in the initial equation until you sabotage it.

There is no special criterion for worthiness. There is no special criterion for one to be wealthy in relationships, to be wealthy in health, or to be rich in monies. There is no chant or dance or special sacrifice that must be made. All has been provided and is at your disposal now, at this moment. You must, however, know that it is available and that your task is possible to see through to fruition, until your desired end is met.

Worthiness drives you beyond any obstacles that you might meet. Worthiness drives you beyond the doubters that all would-be successes have encountered. Worthiness assists you in narrowing your focus, blocking out the noise of failed experiences of others. Where they failed, you will succeed, as long as you believe yourself to be worthy.

Along with your development of worthiness comes possibility. Without worthiness, possibility is shut up behind doors of lack of awareness and disbelief. All that you desire to achieve still exists, and others are partaking of the resources you require now, but a mind that entertains unworthiness and disbelief does not see possibility or options. This mind cannot see beyond the first potential obstacle to getting started and therefore all effort comes to a halt.

Without worthiness there is no possibility. Without possibility there is no hope, and where there is no hope there is no effort.

The finances that you need and desire are a direct reflection of your self-worth. The level on which you exist right now is the level on which you have your mind set.

Key:

Increase your awareness by noticing the massive exchanges of money that occur daily, from which many individuals benefit. Capture the fact that even the most heinous of criminals can attract wealth, so what makes you unworthy? Decide that you are worthy and that you participate in the exchange of wealth throughout the world that occurs at every moment. Decide all things are possible for you, and coat this decision with the fact that the sun rises on all who exist without discrimination, and so the sun will also rise on your finances.

Train To See Opportunities (Problems To Solve)

The problem solver is quietly one of the most well-kept secrets in business and money making. What skills or experiences do you have that could provide support, answer questions, or solve problems for others? What skills or experiences do you have that could provide additional knowledge or education to those coming along the same path as you in a certain area? This could be in relationships, health, finances, spiritually, or in business. It could also be in any of the many subsets or mini areas that fall under the heading of each of these topics.

Begin by training yourself to see opportunities. What problems or challenges do many of your friends or family seem to have in common? The subset of your inner most circle may be a reflection of a much larger group with the same experience, and if you can assist or solve their dilemma, you may now be in a position to create fulfillment and great wealth for yourself.

What are you passionate about? What do you enjoy doing now that you do not get paid for? These are great questions to begin opening your eyes to possibilities and opportunities that exist all around you. Do not fall for the idea that what you know or what you have to offer is unworthy of another person's money. This is a sad mistake that is made every day by the masses. If what you can do or provide is valuable enough to the next person, if it affects their lives in a way that is important to them, they will pay and gladly contribute to your coffers in exchange.

To this point, you have been conditioned and taught to prepare for a job, or to contribute to the expanding of another's enterprise. It is time to shift to the mindset of old. It is time to shift to the mindset of the early settlers who were entrepreneurs, who provided independent value to others in exchange for equivalent value whether it was money or some other form of benefit. If this is not your goal; that which you enjoy could be a magnificent supplement to your primary resources.

8

So what do you enjoy, hunting, fishing, cooking, children, parenting, gardening, lawn care, old cars, restoration of old trinkets, sports, exercise, organic foods, watching television, video games, painting? Are you good at math, science, social studies, or history? Any of these carries the potential to offer a value for value exchange to those in need.

Key:

Become a seer of opportunities. Sharply evaluate the skill sets you have acquired. Notice where your passion lies in life and align the two. Where they meet could be a lucrative point of possibility for you.

Interest – The Use Of Money To Make Money

An interest in the interest calculations of money is a very important part of life in which to play. The workings of the money game in its current flow all over the world must be of great interest to the wealth conscious individual.

For one, the use of money to make money 24 hours a day is a welcoming invitation in itself. For two, the understanding that is required to maintain a clear sense of how and why the movements of money are made or occur is not that difficult. Strength in companies should be of interest. The character of a company should be of interest. The potential reception and outlook of a company should be of interest.

The energetic positioning of a company and its leadership grants insight into its attraction of success and longevity. Just as the energetic positioning of the individual grants insight into his/her attraction of success and longevity. Those who trust in flow, and in Source, and can read its workings in the lives of individuals in physical reality, know that an organization that is grown and developed in the physical reality will proceed the same way, either through associating with the negative lower range energies or the positive higher range energies.

Interest is the calculation of the cost of using someone else's money to further your own causes. This arrangement meets the needs of all parties by returning value to the lender and providing needed value to the borrower. This is the position you place yourself in when purchasing stocks in companies, or buying into funds who purchase stocks from companies. You place yourself in the lenders position, and in position to earn interest on the money you have placed in the care of the companies in which you invest.

No matter what you do, remember, of what you create on your own, you can only exchange so much value for value. Multiple streams of income are necessary to create great wealth and one stream is to position your money to make money in the form of interest.

Get a feel for the game, but remember, the price of money is a lot easier to approach and develop, than to put a price on your time and the experiences you give up having to personally create and exchange value.

Key:

The mechanism and flow of money is a volatile game, but do not let that scare you away. It is also a powerful deliverer of income. Research the purpose of a company, the character of a company, and the potential outlook and acceptance by people of a company. These are enormous indicators as to its potential success and longevity.

Use Of A Budget For Accountability And Increase

Most think of a budget as a means to constrict and hold onto their money out of fear. This is why so many without money or who struggle from a lack of it do not have one. On the contrary, many of the wealthy within your physical existence rely on a budget religiously. They do not rely on it out of fear, but out of respect and responsibility for their money and its proper use. They rely on a budget to hold themselves and others accountable to the highest and best use of the money they have.

First, money is a flowing device. It flows just as the waters flow from one point to the next, from areas of higher elevation to areas of lower elevation, and then it changes forms and returns to the higher elevation from which it started. You must allow money to flow and be a wide conduit to and for its presence. The greater the ease at which you allow money to flow through you the more and stronger the flow will be. This requires the absence of fear of any kind, and the presence of gratitude for its positive nature and the contribution to your life and others.

A budget, allows you to track your transactions and know exactly where your money goes. If monies need to flow through more money making activities you can easily see where changes can be made. If monies need to flow toward charitable activities you can easily shift the flow. It is a matter of choice, but as you build your reservoirs and channel the flow of money through you, it is important to know the directions in which your money flows. This is a position of strength and not weakness. This is an indication of thought and mind, and the position on which you place yourself from a worthiness standpoint.

If you are worthy of money then you stand to command your money and know its reaches into the world. If you are worthy of money, you are aware of the many opportunities to increase its flow and you prepare for them. If you are worthy of money, its presence excites you and you view it as a trusted friend and confidant in the activities of the physical realm.

Your idea of money is the cause of your abundance or your lack of it. Budgeting your money is a grand way to getting on the road to independence mentally and financially.

Key:
Create a budget of each category that currently exists in your spending and each category that you would like to exist. As you create the budget you require for your life and begin the attraction of the resources, your mind must be set on what is required, whether that is $10,000 or $100,000. The subtle forces of the inner realm know not of your needs and desires. They only respond to your thought energy, your subconscious beliefs. With that in mind, you must set your mind on what you require, what you want and intend your life to look like and not what you need at the moment. If you merely focus on what you need, that is all that you will draw into your life.

Drive With Sale Of Service

The sale of your service, if you have taken the time to outline what that is, is the driving force to opening the many financial doors that exist. To the humble, feeble at heart, the sale of a service is a daunting task that borders on an offensive attack on another individual's well-being and comfort. This is so far from the case.

Sales are what drive any and all economies. Sales are the life blood of business. If your company or business made no sales there would be no jobs. Do you feel that your service is saleable? That is the question. Are there people or companies out there that would actually pay for what you have to offer? The good news is that yes, someone will, but you have to make sure that there are enough of those some ones to make your efforts worth your while.

Sale, sale, sale, your service to as many, and through as many channels as you can. Build and grow your efforts to reach new and more potential customers or clients. Get the education you need, uncover the knowledge you require as you attempt to sell, not before. The greatest assimilation of knowledge comes when you are actively engaged in the activity for which the knowledge is required.

Make your service available. Seek out all who could benefit and all who should benefit.

You will encounter obstacles. You will encounter challenges; the biggest of all will be yourself. You have not been groomed for life at the highest level of responsibility. You have not been groomed for a life of negotiation. You have not been groomed for a life of the highest passion, the highest confidence, or the highest self-expression. Therefore you must embrace them quickly and face your fears and your discomfort. You must allow the weakness to ooze from your body as you allow in the strength that so many have and are showing exists.

Build a community of those who share your passion for knowing, and understanding of your service. Create and provide a way for them to communicate with each other, and your base will grow. Love them and they will love you back with their support.

Key:
You have the ability within you to create and swell an economy of your choosing, but you must embrace the strength and courage required to give it life. Although it may need tweaking along the way, the service that ignites your passion also ignites that passion in others in the world. Will you go forth? Will you take the step into the unknown realm of finance creation and money flow? The door is always there, you just have not been trained to see it. Open!

15

Release The Need For $$$$, Exist Outside Of This Belief

The need for money is a false sense of reality that has been created to command and stifle the growth and development of a human being. For years the focus was on the exchange of value and not on the mechanism of exchange. Service for service was exchanged. Goods for services were exchanged. It was never about the mechanism of exchange in and of itself.

Your history clearly shows the time periods where the human race transitioned from being a culture of highly skilled producers and suppliers, to a mass of mere laborers. This has caused the greatest disparity in the distribution of wealth. There will always be those who scale their way to the top through their efforts. But in a community of highly skilled producers and suppliers, no one goes hungry or is poor.

So with this in mind, release the need for money, or better the idea of the need for money. Universal law shows you that those who are not in need attract powerfully what they desire, and the greatest statement of having and surety, the opposite of need and lack, is to give it away. And we do not mean to give it away frivolously; we mean to give it away as guided by spirit in the journey of your life and in the approach of your goals. Give it away in fun and in play, as well as through your service, your business, and the increase of your skill and the service you provide. The individual who gives of their food sustenance is never lacking of food. The individual who gives of their clothing in the aid of others is never without garments of their own. This is because they allow the flow to occur and are a willing participant in propelling the cycle forward.

Think for a moment. Gifts are offered all the time. Cars are offered as gifts. Homes are offered as gifts. Tickets to exotic lands are offered as gifts. This is a normal occurrence that happens in your physical reality everyday. If it is not happening in your personal, individual experience, it is because you do not believe in it and this is directly related to your belief that you need money for all purposes in your life.

You must release that thought of the need for money to survive and give of what you have in your purchases and as charity when spirit guides you, and give freely in Love, surety, and knowing that it will be given back to you because you are a willing vessel for its flow.

Increase your skill in the service you provide. If you do not provide a skill outside of your labor for money begin to investigate what service might fully allow your soul's expression to come forth.

Guided by the ancestors within your soul, you can live a marvelous life of expression, experience, and growth, but you cannot allow your perceived need for money to convolute and conflict with your inner processes and the attractive mechanism that is always at work for you.

Money is not the exchange; it is the mechanism of exchange. The value that you offer, your product or your service is the exchange. The more important it is perceived to be to others the more value you can require for its exchange, the more money you can command.

Key:
Release your need for money. Simply know that it flows and you participate in that flow. Remove yourself from traditional thinking and the movement of the masses by focusing on the value you offer or deliver and not the money you do or do not receive. Majesty is the nature of that which is precious, and you are precious once you see it in yourself and allow it to shine. Trust in the processes of the universe.

Observe, See Wealth

It is absolutely baffling to us that the many forms of wealth that exist in your physical reality go unnoticed. It is also baffling that those who seem to be aware of this wealth and abundance fail to connect the feeling of this presence to every area of life in order to realize abundance individually and personally.

Wealth and abundance exist in all forms throughout the Earth, throughout the universe. There is an abundance of resources to provide energy for the human race for multiple millennia. There is an abundance of every animal, every plant, every tree, of the water, of the potential food supply. Nothing was created in scarcity. Everything was created in abundance, and if you sit quietly and embrace the feeling that arises with the thought of abundance and the multitude that exist of every individual thing, you will begin to experience abundance in your life.

Abundance is openness. It is expansive. It is the recognizing and allowing of immense possibility. It is the knowing that so much exists for all to partake and that there is an endless supply. It is knowing that the flow exist and that you intend and are a willing participant.

Opulence is a beautiful word that encompasses the wealth of all things, and even if you do not know what it means, the word lifts your spirits and your sights to greater and more.

The simple training and effort is to see it everywhere you go, everywhere you are. If you see it and embrace it, it will penetrate your inner being and become a part of you. Your own inner recognition that it does exist and that you are one with it will make it so in your personal reality, in your relationships, in your finances, in your health, in your work life, and spiritually.

Key:

There is no substitute for knowing wealth intimately, and the opportunity to do that is all around you. Breathe it, feel it, smell it, touch it, make it a visceral part of your daily experience and it will flow to you in multiple forms.

Require Beyond Your Position

The mind and thinking are tricky mechanisms. While it appears that you control your conscious thought efforts (appears), your subconscious mind, however, knows not of the physical realm. It only knows what you present to it or allow into it. Repetition creates the disciplines or habits, and the energy/attraction connection is made through the subconscious as well.

The subconscious mind does not know or care about your money. If you tell it there is a problem, it says, "Okay, you like money problems." If you tell it there is an over flow of money, then it says, "Okay, let's find the quickest and fastest way to keep that going."

To truly place yourself in alignment with what you need, you must require more than enough. If you have not noticed your financial/money flow hovers around what you need and less because that is all that you require. It is not all that you see as possible, but it is all that you require.

Your subconscious mind must believe that you require a specific amount that is more than what you need in order to be positioned for increase and excess. In your mind right now you have a clear idea of how much money you need for the month, this very idea must be more. It must represent a number higher than what you actually need if you want to experience excess or an abundance of disposable income and not just enough income.

To do this, set your sights on a bigger purpose than just serving yourself. Move yourself mentally out of survival mode and into supplier mode. See yourself as the go to person for your family, for your community, for your town, for your city, for your country. See yourself as the major contributor to a favorite charity. You must require more.

If you budget, and you should, categorize what you intend and would like to do, and make its funding a living required part of your budget. It must be as big a part as paying your light or water bill.

There can be no exceptions, no excuses. It has to be there. You cannot accept anything less.

When you impress upon your subconscious mind that this is your reality, and necessary parts of your reality, your subconscious mind begins to formulate a way, and the way will appear in front of you, just as the way has always and continues to appear in front of you for the position in which you stand today.

Key:
Make your numbers absolute. Make your requirements nonnegotiable. Burn them into the reservoirs of your subconscious mind and allow it to do its work. What you require is what will be. It always has been.

Partner To Expand Ideas And Services Beyond Yourself

Expansion, the want and need to expand is a normal and natural desire. It is a process in nature that is facilitated by the animals, by the wind, by the rain, by insects, and by human beings. Basically, every living and nonliving entity participates in the coordination of expansion. Seeds can travel to distant lands. Animals can find home in remote locations. Anything and everything is possible.

The growth and expansion of your idea is no different. Partnership with individuals or entities who are excited about helping you spread your idea into the world is a grand mechanism for growth. The degree of separation between you and the other side of the world is very small, although incomprehensible to the physical eye. The connections that lie through a person you meet could be astounding. The opportunities that lie through the next scheduled engagement could be beyond imagination. So much more can be achieved when you enlist others to assist you in expansion, it can be scary.

To what do you owe this opportunity? Nothing. You merely must participate in the process that exists as a natural and normal part of nature. Its facilitation cannot be bridled by any one person. Its power cannot be hindered by any one person. It is simply up to you to create the wave, to initiate the ripple in the ocean of possibility. Do not worry about backlash. Do not allow fear to back your efforts for all ripples eventually make their way back to their source.

Offer up your most inspired ideas. Offer up your most impassioned opportunity. The life and energy that you provide is enough propulsion to send your idea into the stratosphere, but you must trust it.

Partnership is a powerful opportunity if you embrace it. No great person in history has had his or her work expand the globe based on their sole efforts. They all received help along the way from those who were inspired. This is a truth.

Key:

Recognize the power of relationship and partnership. Develop them both as often as you can for the benefit and reward can be beyond imagination. Use of this powerful tool requires your effort in the initial as startup force, but beyond that, the wave will travel at infinitum.

Set Your Mind On Your Financial Goal Excluding Everything Else – Follow The Signs

A goal is the intended creation of an experience. Its presence in time and space is a potential manifestation of an individual until they connect it to reason for its existence. It must be connected to a purpose for life.

What goals do you have in plan, in motion at the moment? Are they singular? Are they clear? Do they exist as absolutes, with the full commitment of all of your mental and emotional energy? This is a must for the pull to be established.

Your financial goals are no different than any other goal. They must be established in lieu of knowing fully how they are going to be accomplished; however, their materialization must be a forgone conclusion.

Finances take on a life of their own due to the emotional attachment that is given to them by human beings. To cling, hold onto something, or be fierce in your possession of something is a clear indication of your fear or belief in the lack of it. This sets you apart from it in the beginning. This is a position of weakness.

Release the emotional attachment you carry toward money. Your finances must operate independently of your emotion in order to see them clearly and decide their distribution wisely. Emotion is a high octane fuel that gives life to any current applied to a thought or idea whether it is positive or negative in nature.

Your goal must be the only option, and once this is the decision, the signs in your experience will be made available. The sight you require for opportunity and choice to approach your goal will be made clear. The options you require for materialization will be made obvious along the path of your journey.

Key:

Outline your goal and the life effects that it will have. Pay close attention to the passion that is created. Pay close attention to the sense of fulfillment, due to the accomplishment of your financial goal. This provides the fuel. Make your goal an absolute must for your life. Know that it exists in full completion now.

In Spirit I Thrive, In Mind I Fall. It Is My Job, To Unify Them All.

I now realize that for two decades I have been striving to release the true, authentic me that had been covered by fear-based ideas and perceptions. (Get Past Yourself)

I am realizing that the life I once lived, and the life story that is being lived around me by family and friends is not a chosen life, but one that has been passed along. With elements of fear at its base, loss, pain, failure, and the embarrassment of mistake once defined me, now they propel me. (The Other Side Of Fear)

Now I strive to allow the true, authentic, Source inspired me to breathe through at every moment. This grants me the knowing that my desires are pure and in line with the path that is specifically for me. (Allowing Me)

I did not need a teacher, a preacher, or a guru. All I needed was some Guidance and some Direction. (My Only Need)

Benny

The Rest Of The Series

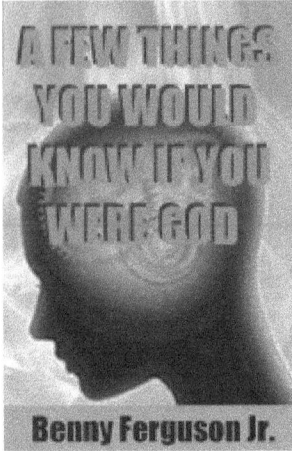

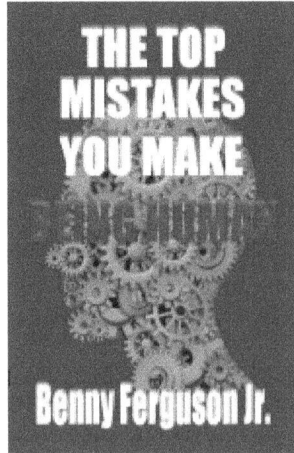

Connecting With Benny:

Facebook: www.facebook.com/bennyrfergusonjr

Youtube: www.youtube.com/BennyFergusonJr/videos

Twitter: www.twitter.com/BennyRFergusonJ

Contacting Benny:

Initial contacts to Benny for discussions, interviews, one – on - one or group coaching, speaking or training may be made through telephone or email.

Phone: 336-546-7142

Email: BennyFerguson@TheFergusonCompany.com